A Friend for Ben

Jeanette McMahon
Illustrated by Marla Baggetta

Rigby

A Harcourt Achieve Imprint

www.Rigby.com
1-800-531-5015

Today was Ben's first day at Evergreen Elementary School, and he was nervous. He didn't want to go to a new school. He missed his old school friends already. He wasn't even interested in eating breakfast.

It looked like it was going to rain, so Ben's mom pulled into a parking spot near the front door of the school.

"Excuse me, but you can't park here," a crossing guard said. "This spot is reserved for Eric."

Ben wondered who Eric was and what made him so special.

The bell rang, and Ben entered his new third grade classroom. It looked a lot like his old classroom. Mrs. Collins, his teacher, introduced Ben to several other students, and then she turned to another woman.

"This is Mrs. Lopez," Mrs. Collins said. "She helps Eric."

Ben wondered again what was so special about Eric.

"And this is Eric," Mrs. Lopez said.

Ben turned to meet his new classmate.
Eric was about the same size as Ben. He
was wearing a blue football shirt, and he was
sitting in a wheelchair.

"Nice to meet you," Eric said.

Eric's words were a little hard for Ben to understand.

"Eric has cerebral palsy," Mrs. Lopez said. "His muscles don't always move the way he wants and he speaks slowly, but Eric always has a lot to say."

Then Mrs. Collins said, "It's writing time, class."

The students began to write in their journals. Ben noticed that Eric used a special computer. He wondered what Eric was writing about.

Afterward some of the students shared their writing. Eric's piece was about his dog, Sport, who can pick up things for Eric and even open doors. Ben liked Eric's story a lot. He thought it would be really fun to have a dog like Sport.

Soon it was time for gym, and Ben was surprised to see that Eric was going to gym, too. Mrs. Lopez pushed Eric's wheelchair down the hall. All of the other students smiled and waved at him. It seemed like everybody knew Eric.

The gym teacher saw Ben.

"Welcome to Evergreen School, Bob," the gym teacher said.

Ben's face turned red.

"His name is Ben," said a voice.

Ben turned around and saw Eric smiling at him.

The class was going to play kickball. Ben
had been the best pitcher in his class at his old
school, and he hoped to pitch today.

Just then Mrs. Lopez pushed Eric's wheelchair
onto the gym floor.

"Eric is the all-time pitcher," a boy whispered
to Ben.

"How can he do that?" Ben asked.

"Just watch," the boy answered.

Eric leaned over the side of his
wheelchair and pitched with his right arm.
"He's pretty good," Ben said.

Later that day when the students lined up to go outside for recess, Eric stayed at his desk and took out a deck of cards.

"Eric needs to stay inside when it's too wet or cold out," a girl told Ben.

Ben wouldn't mind staying inside. He loved to play cards. His favorite game was Crazy Eights.

At the end of the school day, Ben couldn't remember which cubby was his, so he waited until the other students left. Then he spotted his backpack. Suddenly, he heard a voice.

"Could you get my backpack, too?" the voice asked slowly.

It was Eric.

Ben handed Eric his backpack. He didn't know what to say. Just then Mrs. Lopez came in.

"How nice of you to help," she said to Ben. "I was looking for a special helper for Eric. How would you like the job?"

"Do you like to play cards?" Eric
asked Ben.

"Yes," said Ben. "What's your favorite game?"

"I'm crazy about Crazy Eights," Eric said with
a great big smile.